AF269744

The Kids' Guide to Government

How the Executive Branch Works

Zelda Wagner

Lerner Publications ◆ Minneapolis

Lerner Publications Company
An imprint of Lerner Publishing Group, Inc.
241 First Avenue North
Minneapolis, MN 55401 USA

For reading levels and more information, look up this title at www.lernerbooks.com.

Main body text set in Adrianna Regular.
Typeface provided by Chank.

Library of Congress Cataloging-in-Publication Data

Names: Wagner, Zelda, 2000– author.
Title: How the executive branch works / Zelda Wagner.
Description: Minneapolis, MN : Lerner Publications, [2025] | Series: Searchlight books. The kids' guide to government | Includes bibliographical references and index. | Audience: Ages 8–11 | Audience: Grades 4–6 | Summary: "The executive branch is more than just the president. It has departments, agencies, and commissions that help the president run the country. Young readers discover how a large team puts policies into action"— Provided by publisher.
Identifiers: LCCN 2023040531 (print) | LCCN 2023040532 (ebook) | ISBN 9798765626603 (library binding) | ISBN 9798765629611 (paperback) | ISBN 9798765637128 (epub)
Subjects: LCSH: Presidents—United States—Juvenile literature. | Administrative agencies—United States—Juvenile literature. | Executive power—United States— Juvenile literature. | Separation of powers—United States—Juvenile literature.
Classification: LCC JK517 .W344 2025 (print) | LCC JK517 (ebook) | DDC 352.230973— dc23/eng/20230911

LC record available at https://lccn.loc.gov/2023040531
LC ebook record available at https://lccn.loc.gov/2023040532

Manufactured in the United States of America
1-1009928-51991-10/31/2023

Table of Contents

Chapter 1

THE EXECUTIVE BRANCH

During his first full day in office in January 2021, President Joe Biden signed several executive orders. These documents affect the US government and what it can do. One order he signed declared the US would rejoin the Paris Agreement.

This agreement states that nations around the globe will release fewer greenhouse gases, or gases that trap heat, into Earth's atmosphere. This will help slow down climate change. Biden believed joining this project with other countries would help protect our planet. The US Constitution gives the president the power to sign executive orders like this one.

President Biden signing an executive order on his first day in office

Three Branches

The US government has three branches. They are the executive, legislative, and judicial branches. The branches work together to make laws for citizens to follow. The Constitution defines the jobs of each branch.

The main job of the executive branch is to make sure laws are followed. The president leads this branch. The president signs laws written by Congress in the legislative branch. The president can also sometimes veto, or stop, a bill that Congress has passed. But the bill

Democrats talk on the floor in the House of Representatives.

Vice President Kamala Harris giving a speech

can go through Congress again and pass if two-thirds of Congress agrees to support it.

The vice president has the second-highest position in the executive branch. The vice president works for the president. One duty is to attend events with the Senate. They can also vote to break a tie in the Senate. The vice president takes over as president if the president can't finish their term.

The executive branch includes other groups that help carry out laws. One group is the president's cabinet.

President Donald Trump speaks to his advisers during a cabinet meeting.

These people are advisers to the president. Executive departments and federal agencies help the president carry out laws as well.

One Leader, Many Roles

The president has many roles. The president has some power over how the country manages its money. They give ideas to Congress on where money should go over the next year. Another role the president has is to represent the United States to the world. They meet with foreign leaders.

Democracy and You

People send letters to presidents for many reasons. You can send a letter to the president if you're concerned about an issue, such as climate change or immigration. You can send a letter in response to something the president did recently. People who work for the president read these letters. Sometimes they pass letters along to the president. The president might send a response back. No matter what, you have a voice.

The president must work with both the legislative and judicial branches to make decisions. The founders of the country wrote the Constitution this way. They didn't want one branch of government to have too much power. This is called a system of checks and balances. The three branches of government balance one another.

President George W. Bush (*right*) shaking hands with British Prime Minister Gordon Brown (*left*) in 2008

LEADING THE COUNTRY

A candidate for president must follow certain constitutional rules. A president must be a citizen of the US at birth. The president must be at least thirty-five years old.

Congress limits the number of years a president can be in office. The president's term is four years. The president can serve two terms. In the past, a president

President Barack Obama served two terms as the US president.

could serve unlimited terms. But in 1951, Congress passed the Twenty-Second Amendment. It placed a term limit on future presidents.

The vice president is also elected to a term of four years. But vice presidents can serve any number of years and under different presidents. The vice president can also choose to run for president after finishing their term as vice president.

A Trusted Team

To do their job, the president needs the help of other people. These people make up the president's administration. They should be experts in their fields. The president chooses them carefully. One important leader is the White House chief of staff. This person manages the president's office. They make sure the rest of the White House staff are doing their jobs well.

RON KLAIN WAS PRESIDENT BIDEN'S
CHIEF OF STAFF FROM 2020 TO 2022.

When a new president enters office, a new administration enters too. The president chooses possible people for the administration. The president selects US ambassadors to serve in other countries. The president also chooses possible federal judges and justices of the Supreme Court. All these people require the Senate's approval.

President Trump nominates Amy Coney Barrett to the Supreme Court on September 26, 2020.

Deep Dive

In February 2022, Biden announced his nomination of Judge Ketanji Brown Jackson to the Supreme Court. She went through confirmation hearings before the Senate Judicial Committee. They asked her questions about her work experiences. They looked into her background to make sure she was fit for the job. Then the Senate voted on whether to accept Biden's nomination. They confirmed her with a 53–47 vote. Jackson was sworn into office on June 30, 2022. She is the first Black woman on the US Supreme Court.

ADVISING THE PRESIDENT

The Constitution set up the executive cabinet. Cabinet members help the president make decisions. The idea of a cabinet dates back to George Washington's presidency. Back then, only three executive departments—state, war, and treasury—were in charge of certain tasks.

These days, the president's cabinet has fifteen departments that perform specific jobs. Some work with education policies, while others work with health and human services in the US. The cabinet also includes the vice president and the attorney general. The attorney general represents the US in legal matters and gives legal advice to the president.

Secretary of Education Miguel Cardona speaks during a briefing at the White House in 2023.

Deep Dive

The secretary of education advises the president on decisions about schools. One decision was the No Child Left Behind Act. President George W. Bush signed it into law in 2002. His secretary of education, Rod Paige, advised him on the decision. The government had noticed that some children got a better education than others did. The goal of the No Child Left Behind Act was to give every child a good education. The act set up standardized tests to measure schools' success. In 2015 President Barack Obama replaced it with the Every Student Succeeds Act.

The head of each department is the secretary. The president calls on secretaries for their opinions on important issues. The secretary of state, for example, advises the president and carries out foreign policy. Foreign policy includes the actions the US takes with other countries, such as buying goods and bringing them to the US. Between 2021 and 2022, the secretary of state visited more than fifty countries.

Protecting Resources

The secretary of the treasury helps the president with economic issues. They manage money and advise the president on policies that affect how money flows through society. The department includes the Bureau of Engraving and Printing and the US Mint. The US Mint designs and produces money. Alexander Hamilton was the first secretary of the treasury.

Secretary of the Treasury Janet Yellen prepares for a panel discussion at the 2023 Summit for Democracy.

Bryan Todd Newland during his confirmation hearing to become Assistant Secretary of the Bureau of Indian Affairs

The Department of the Interior protects natural resources. The National Park Service is in this department. It was formed in 1916. The US has more than sixty official national parks and hundreds of national park sites.

Another part is the Bureau of Indian Affairs. It works for the interests of Native Americans. Its job includes protecting Native American lands.

Staying Safe

Some cabinet departments protect the United States. One of these is the military. The secretary of defense manages the military. The military has six branches. The army is the oldest and largest. The navy and the marine corps were created next. The newest branches are the coast guard, air force, and space force.

MEMBERS OF THE MARINE CORPS UNDERGO INTENSE TRAINING.

The Department of Homeland Security protects the United States from people or things that might harm the US. It watches the borders closely. This department is also in charge of many immigration policies. An informal office of homeland security formed after terrorists attacked the US on September 11, 2001. This office officially became the Department of Homeland Security in 2003.

Chapter 4

EXECUTIVE WORK

Hundreds of agencies do the executive branch's work. They help carry out decisions made by the department secretaries and apply them to daily life.

Protecting the Country

One of these agencies is the Central Intelligence Agency. Its role is to collect information. The agency learns about threats to the United States. It takes direction from the president.

Another agency is the Environmental Protection Agency. Its job is to protect the environment. This agency creates rules for people and companies to keep the air, land, and water clean.

The National Archives and Records Administration manages presidential libraries. It also preserves US government records. It takes special care of the

Michael Regan (*middle*) was the first Black man to become administrator of the Environmental Protection Agency in 2021.

The Constitution and the Bill of Rights on display at the National Archives Museum

founding documents. The Declaration of Independence, the Constitution, and the Bill of Rights are on display in the National Archives Museum in Washington, DC.

Progress in Science and Peace

The National Science Foundation was formed in 1950. It helps raise money for important research at American colleges and universities. Their findings help science progress.

Peace Corps volunteers travel to other countries. They help with education, health, and training. The idea for this agency came in 1960. Massachusetts senator John F. Kennedy spoke at the University of Michigan. He asked ten thousand students if they were willing to serve their country in the name of peace. Many said yes. As president, Kennedy signed a bill establishing the Peace Corps in 1961.

First Lady Michelle Obama (*second from left*) at a Peace Corps training center in 2016

Mail carriers get letters and packagers where they need to go.

Mail Delivery

The US Postal Service delivers mail to your home. Its mission is to provide fast and affordable mail service. Mail gets delivered, no matter where people live.

Running the Country

The executive branch is more than just the president. It has many people who help run the country. It has departments and agencies who work together with other parts of government. It takes a team to lead a nation. One day, you or someone close to you could be a part of the president's team.

What Do You Think?

At seventy-seven, Biden was the oldest president elected to office. Presidents have a minimum age requirement, but they don't have a maximum age limit. Some people think the government should place a limit on how old a person can be to become president.

Some voters want a younger president that will share younger people's concerns. Others think an older president will have more wisdom and experience to guide the country.

Do you think the president should have an age limit? Why or why not?

Glossary

administration: the people working in the executive branch under a president

adviser: someone who gives advice

ambassador: a representative of a nation

bill: a proposed piece of law

citizen: a person who lives in a country and receives protection from their government

climate change: a significant and long-lasting change in Earth's climate and weather patterns

economic: having to do with the economy, or the sale and purchase of goods and services

federal: relating to the national government

immigration: moving to a different country

nomination: naming a person to an office or role

policy: a set of rules about what should be done

terrorist: a person who uses violence to achieve a goal, usually for political reasons

Learn More

Ben's Guide to the US Government
   https://bensguide.gpo.gov

BrainPOP: Executive Command
   https://www.brainpop.com/games/executivecommand/

Kiddle: Executive Order Facts for Kids
   https://kids.kiddle.co/Executive_order

Stratton, Connor. *President*. Lake Elmo, MN: Focus Readers, 2024.

Tyner, Dr. Artika R. *Black Achievements in Politics: Celebrating Shirley Chisholm, Barack Obama, and More*. Minneapolis: Lerner Publications, 2024.

Wagner, Zelda. *How the Judicial Branch Works*. Minneapolis: Lerner Publications, 2025.

Index

Photo Acknowledgments

Image credits: The White House/Adam Schultz, pp. 5, 13; Jabin Botsford/The Washington Post via Getty Images, p. 6; AP Photo/Patrick Semansky, p. 7; AP Photo/Pablo Martinez Monsivais, p. 8; AP Photo/Lawrence Jackson, p. 10; AP Photo/Jae C. Hong, p. 12; Ken Cedeno/Sipa via AP, p. 14; AP Photo/Susan Walsh, p. 17; Roy Rochlin/Getty Images, p. 19; AP Photo/Andrew Harnik, p. 20; Graeme Sloan/Sipa via AP Images, p. 21; U.S. Marine Corps/Lance Cpl. Averi Rowton, p. 22; Scott Varley/Digital First Media/Torrance Daily Breeze via Getty Images, p. 23; Eric Lee/Bloomberg via Getty Images, p. 25; Carol M. Highsmith/Buyenlarge/Getty Images, p. 26; Walter Rodriguez/Alamy, p. 27; EQRoy/Shutterstock, p. 28.

Cover: The White House/Adam Schultz.